Your Daughter's

D0716428

from confetti.co.uk
don't let your daughter get
married without us...

First published in 2003 by Octopus Publishing Group,
2–4 Heron Quays, London, E14 4JP
www.conran-octopus.co.uk
Reprinted in 2005

A catalogue record for this book is available
from the British Library.

ISBN 184091 306 1

Publishing Director Lorraine Dickey
Senior Editor Katey Day
Assistant Editor Sybella Marlow
Creative Director Leslie Harrington
Designer Jeremy Tilston
Senior Production Controller Manjit Sihra

Contents

YOUR DAUGHTER'S WEDDING

Your daughter has finally found the man of her dreams. You're ecstatic, of course, but the butterflies have already started. Never mind her dress, what on earth will you wear and how will you get everything arranged in time?

Traditionally this is your chance to shine (or not) as a hostess. But have things changed? Exactly what role does a modern-day mother of the bride play? Do you just turn up on the day and smile? Or are you in for months of planning and preparation?

Relax, confetti.co.uk is here to help...

What do I do?

If you're playing by the traditional rules
(and plenty do), the bride's mother:

- Helps finalize the guest list (degree in
  diplomacy preferable)
- Orders the stationery (invitations, menus,
  order of service, place cards)
- Sends out the invitations and
  monitors replies
- Supplies copies of the gift list on request

YOUR DAUGHTER'S WEDDING

- Arranges and books the reception (liaising constantly with the couple, if your life is worth living)
- Hires the cars
- Organizes the flowers for the church, reception and the bride's bouquet
- Books the photographer (avoiding control freaks who'll take over)
- Draws up the seating plan (again and again)
- And generally acts as the official hostess with the most-est

But it doesn't have to be that way…

I'M IN CHARGE... AREN'T I?

Modern mums of the bride...
- Listen to the couple's views
- Make endless lists of what is needed
- Lie convincingly when the bride asks:
'Do you mind if we marry
abroad/elope/don't have bridesmaids'?
- Wait to be asked before getting involved!

Modern mums of the bride also...

- Don't interfere if their daughter insists on doing everything herself
- Give their daughter away themselves (with or without their husband)
- Make speeches at the reception
- Go on the hen night or plan one for their daughter
- Choose not to wear a hat

Real MoBs:

A break from tradition

'My daughter won't touch fruitcake so we had chocolate cake instead. One layer was dark, one milk chocolate and one white chocolate. I was terrified it would melt, but it was fine and the guests loved it.'

Tips for taking charge: 1

Suggest you and your daughter sit down
and make a list of everything there is to do.
Once she's seen the long list of jobs, she
might be delighted to delegate!

For a full personalized to-do list, with
weekly reminders, see the confetti.co.uk
planning tools at
www.confetti.co.uk/weddings
/planning_tools/default.asp

Tips for taking charge: 2

Do the engaged couple a big favour and suggest that before they formally announce the date, you check the availability of their chosen venues, band, caterers and key guests!

Need a venue? Look here first
www.confetti.co.uk/venues/default.asp

Tips for taking charge: 3

Mothers of the groom might wish to get involved, which can sometimes cause tension. Easy ways to involve the in-laws include asking her to make the cake, organize the food for the evening reception or arrange the flowers.

confetti.co.uk can help you find a photographer, DJ, mobile bar, dressmaker…
Just log on to
www.confetti.co.uk/confetti_pages
/default.asp

Real MoBs:
A joint project

'My daughter was adamant she'd do all the planning, but with her busy job, it just wasn't possible. In the end it was a joint project, and we're closer for it.'

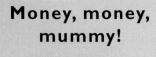

Money, money, mummy!

Who pays for what?

Traditionally the bride's parents pay for the stationery, bride's and bridesmaid's dresses, cars, cake, flowers, music, photography and the reception.

The groom pays for the rings, ceremony fees, his clothes, transport for himself and the best man, gifts for the best man and bridesmaids and the honeymoon.

Who pays for what?

…but these days, it's quite common for the couple or even the groom's parents to want to contribute.

The more the merrier

…and the more bankrupt you'll be at the end of it. Set a guest-list limit based on a specific budget. But remember, not everyone will be able to come, so a few extra won't matter.

Be upfront

If you're dishing out the dough for the main event, it's only fair to tell the couple at an early stage how much money there is to play with.

Budget online

It's all too easy for costs to escalate, so keep control with a free wedding budget planner:
www.confetti.co.uk/weddings /planning_tools/default.asp

Spend where it matters

Early on, get the bride and groom to decide
what's really important to them. If they've
always dreamt of a having a jazz band, cut
back somewhere else.

www.confetti.co.uk/weddings/default.asp
will provide you with more inspired
money-saving ideas.

Beg, steal or borrow

Ask your friends. You could ask a mate to make the cake, for example, or a relative with a classic car to get them to the church. Be careful with amateur photographers, however – those snaps have to last a lifetime.

Double up with disposable cameras for the guests – you can match yours to your colour theme at www.confetti.co.uk/shopping/default.asp

Creative accounting

Hotels can prove expensive for receptions.
Why not try somewhere different – your
local zoo, college or even your
own garden?

Need to cut costs?

What about canapes or a buffet spread rather than a sit-down meal? Or invite some people to the evening reception, rather than to the full wedding.

Check what's included

Does the quote from the reception venue include VAT? Will the hotel charge extra for table flowers, a cake knife or a room for the bride and groom to change in? Watch out for corkage charges if you're bringing your own champagne.

For a comprehensive checklist go to www.confetti.co.uk/confetti_pages/checklists /default.asp

Real MoBs:

Cake con

'The hotel tried to charge us £20 just
to use their cake knife. It was a real con, so
we refused to pay that part of the bill.'

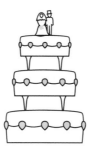

Cover yourself

Take out wedding insurance. It will cover you against those nightmare scenarios such as the wedding venue being double-booked.

Real MoBs:

Photo finish

'We paid out for a professional photographer, but arranged for our friend to do the video, which kept costs down.'

Dress to impress

Anything goes

No idea what to wear? Don't worry.
These days there are no formal rules:
just don't upstage the bride.

Flaunt your assets

…but hide your flaws is the best rule of thumb. Wear what you love and what looks good on you.

Shop till you drop
Finding the right outfit is all part of the fun.
Enjoy! You've never had such a good
excuse to buy that Gucci bag.

Hats off

To wear a hat or not to wear a hat?
It's up to you. If hats don't suit you,
silk flowers in your hair can look
just as chic.

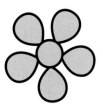

DRESS TO IMPRESS

Picture perfect

Think about how you want to be seen and
remembered on your daughter's big day.
Beautiful, elegant, chic, youthful,
trendy, modern?

Disco diva

If there's an evening do, how will your outfit look then? Can you dance in it? Will you need a jacket? A long jacket over a shift dress may be the answer. Or even a change of clothes.

Will you clash?

Liaise with the groom's mother about her outfit. You don't want to look the same, or clash! It's a good excuse for a getting-to-know-you phone call, or even a joint shopping trip.

Real MoBs:

Nicely groomed

'The groom's mum and I got together for a trying-on session to check our outfits went together. We had such a laugh we're now great friends and regularly shop together.'

New shoes?

Wear your shoes in before the wedding
day – you'll be on your feet for most of it.
And it's a good idea to carry a couple of
spare plasters in your handbag, just in
case of emergencies.

Bags of space

Accessories can make or break an outfit.
But make sure the handbag you choose to
take has space for a lot of tissues!
You could also carry make-up essentials
for the bride.

Real MoBs:

Suit yourself!

'Why wear a dress? I never normally do and my daughter's wedding was no exception. I bought some designer trousers and a jacket. I'd have felt dreadful in a dress.'

She's coming.
End of discussion.

SHE'S COMING. END OF DISCUSSION.

Traditionally...

The bride's parents hosted the wedding and so drew up the guest list, organized the printing of the invitations and sent them out at least six weeks before the big day.

Today, it's usually a joint decision...
So, start with the absolute must-haves like
family members, ushers and bridesmaids.
The rest of the list needs tactful negotiation
between you, your daughter and her fiancé.

Guest stress

'She'll never speak to me again if we don't invite her!' Cool it. Remember this is your daughter's wedding, for her and the groom's friends and family.

Auntie who?

The last time you saw her was at your daughter's christening, so does Auntie So-and-So really need an invitation? But if you feel guilty, send her some wedding cake afterwards.

SHE'S COMING. END OF DISCUSSION.

Too many friends?

The answer is to have an evening do and invite them to that. Your daughter can do the same with her office crowd if inviting them all to the wedding would blow the budget.

Numbers too high?

Cut out the kids. Drop a note in with the invitations to parents saying: 'Much as we'd love to invite all our friends' children, it is only possible to accommodate children of close family.'

All your invitation queries answered at www.confetti.co.uk/invitations/default.asp

SHE'S COMING. END OF DISCUSSION.

Wording worries

The usual invitation wording is:

Mr and Mrs Jonathan Jones
request the pleasure of your company
at the marriage of their daughter
Sarah
to Mr James Bond
at St Mary's Church, Milton,
on (date, month, year),
at (time),
and afterwards at (reception location).
RSVP (hosts' address).

Divorce dilemma

If you are divorced or separated, the easiest way to word the invite is to simply include both your full names, to underline that you are individuals:

'Mr Jonathan Jones and Mrs Jane Jones (or other surname if remarried) request the pleasure, etc'. Or the invitation can come solely from you!

SHE'S COMING. END OF DISCUSSION.

Keep them informed

Along with the invitation, guests will need directions to the venues, information on overnight accommodation and gift list details. You may prefer to wait until asked before you send out the gift list.

Real MoBs:

Ring around

'My daughter and I phoned round the principal people to tell them the wedding date months in advance. It meant the people we really, really wanted were able to come.'

Real MoBs:

Fair's fair

'The two families reached deadlock over the guest list, as we have barely any relatives but the groom's family is huge. In the end, we compromised by agreeing on a fixed number of guests for each set of parents.'

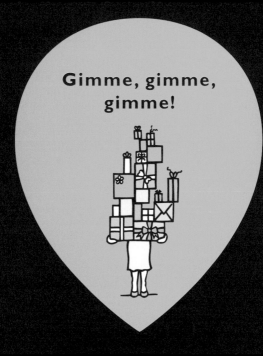

Not another toaster!

Gift lists avoid the problem of ending up with duplicate presents, so encourage your daughter and her fiancé to have one.

Rude to ask?

It's fairly normal practice now to send gift lists out with the invitations. But if you don't feel comfortable doing this, one way round it is to put the gift list online and simply include the Internet address. You can do this at www.confetti.co.uk

Real MoBs:

Easy pieces

'My daughter felt awkward asking for big-ticket items, so her gift list divided the sofa she wanted into pieces. Guests could buy a cushion, leg, right-hand seat, etc. Everyone loved the idea'!

Prices to please

Check your daughter's gift list contains a
big range of products at different prices.
For guests there's nothing worse than
finding they can't afford to buy anything
on the list.

MoB bullying!

Gently encourage people you know well to buy from the list, so the couple get at least some of the items they want. Ask your daughter which presents she most wants so you can suggest people buy these first.

Eye on the list

Keep checking the list to ensure there are still gifts left to purchase. The bride may need to add more items, especially in the mid-price range. It's worth adding some last minute extras for the disorganized!

They've got it all

If this is your daughter's second marriage or she's been living with her partner for some time, they may already have everything for the house. But modern wedding gift lists can include just about anything from a scuba-diving course or spa treatment to salsa dance classes.

They've got it all

The list doesn't need to be all unpatterned china and white bedlinen. It's OK for your daughter to stamp her personality on her list. See www.confetti.co.uk/giftlist/default.asp for alternative and interesting ideas.

Real MoBs:
Get creative

'My daughter remarried at 35 and didn't really need anything for the house. But we soon came up with things she wanted, like a luxury picnic basket and photo frames for her wedding pictures.'

No time to compile a list?

If your daughter is too busy to compile a list, confetti.co.uk's gift list service can help. She can do it from home, using confetti.co.uk's wedding book with 1,500 products, or set up a personalized wedding web page using confetti.co.uk's website.

What can we give them?

Traditionally, parents buy the larger items on the list, such as a dishwasher or fridge freezer. But modern mothers of the bride might prefer to buy them a weekend away, their going away outfits or maybe a piece of jewellery.

Flowers and photos

Who pays for the flowers?

The groom traditionally pays for the bride's bouquet, but the parents of the bride are left to pick up the bill for the rest: church and reception flowers and buttonholes.

Flowers can cost the earth!

Two ways to make savings are to use arrangements already in the church or reception venue, or share with another couple getting married at the same venue that weekend. However, bear in mind you'll need to reach a joint agreement on colour schemes.

Real MoBs:

Silk saved the day

'We didn't have to spend money on flowers
at our daughter's reception as they already
had beautiful silk flower arrangements in
place from a previous function.'

What's that, petal?

If floristry isn't your daughter's strong
point, offer her some support and advice
on what to include in her bouquet and any
arrangements she's having in the church.

Find a florist

If you don't know a florist, go on personal recommendation. Most florists can show you and the bride pictures of wedding arrangements, but don't be afraid to ask for something more unusual.

Seasonal sense

Take the florist's advice on what flowers
will be in season – they'll be cheaper too!
Bear in mind that some flowers can stain
and others can make you sneeze.

Collect and deliver
Don't forget to organize how the flowers
will be collected on the day – corsages
might need to be brought to the house,
for example.

Book the best

Wedding pictures are priceless – you can never replace them, so make sure the bride and groom book the best, even if it costs you an arm and a leg.

Picture perfect

Check the photographer's portfolio and find out what sort of pictures he or she can take. If the couple want black-and-white pictures or reportage shots, is this something he or she can do? What about digital photography, saved on CD?

How many pictures are included as standard? Will the couple get an album? Does the quote include VAT?

Snap-happy!

Provide disposable cameras on each reception table. That way guests can take some informal shots of people enjoying themselves. Just make sure you collect the cameras at the end!

And action!

Check whether the couple want a video
record of their wedding day.
If a professional video company is too
pricey, ask a friend with a camcorder if they
would mind lending it to you for the day.

Video nasty

If you hire a professional to shoot the video or DVD, find out what's included in the price. Extra charges may be made for editing and dubbing music.

Real MoBs:

Trigger happy

'My daughter got so fed up with the photographer pushing her and the groom around, she told him she was going to be sick and refused to have any more pictures taken.'

Who travels with whom?
The bride leaves last, usually with her father
or whoever is giving her away. You and the
bridesmaids traditionally travel together
in another car, while the best man is
responsible for getting the groom
to the ceremony venue on time.

Classic choice

Vintage cars may be the classic choice, but just about any mode of transport is acceptable these days, from helicopters to hot-air balloons or even the local bus.

Uniform look

If you're using a chauffeur-driven service, find out if the driver will be wearing a uniform on the day. Make sure this and the colour of the car don't clash with the bride or bridesmaid's dresses, groom's outfit, flowers and so on.

Something a bit different

Make sure the bride and groom have considered the practicalities of their chosen transport. A pony and trap may be fine in summer, but will be freezing cold in winter. A dramatic entrance or exit by helicopter may be exciting, but will those rotor blades ruin the bride's hair?

Real MoBs:

All white on the day

'Our daughter chose a white London taxi for her wedding. It was a lot cheaper than a limousine and there was plenty of room in the back for her long train.'

Check the charges

Find out how the transport costs will be calculated. Are you paying by the hour or distance and is there a minimum charge? Pay a deposit and confirm in writing. Double-check your booking!

Beg, steal or borrow

If the plan is to borrow a posh car
from a friend, make sure the car is
cleaned and beribboned beforehand.

Getting the guests there

Consider your guests' needs. Will they all have cars, or do you need to organize lifts for some people?

First night hotel transport

Don't forget to organize the bride and groom's means of escape if they're travelling on to a hotel for the night.

TOO CHICKEN FOR THE HEN NIGHT?

Who plans the hen night?

The chief bridesmaid normally takes on this job. But modern brides often have more than one party.

Should I be invited?

It all depends on how practical it is. If a wild girly night at a club isn't your scene, then probably not. But if your daughter's planning a day out at a spa, she may want to include you. Wait to be asked!

Real MoBs:

And for my third hen night
'My daughter had three hen nights – one
for her friends in London, one for her
college mates and one staying in our
cottage in France with her sister and me.'

Organize something yourself

Modern mothers of the bride may want to organize a meal or weekend away with their daughter.

Organize something yourself
It's the perfect time to discuss those last minute details for the wedding. There are loads of ideas on the confetti.co.uk website.

Brides abroad

'That's wonderful darling!'
…is the correct reply to 'We're getting
married abroad', however many misgivings
you may have about it. After all, it's a great
excuse for a holiday, if you're invited.
And if not, you can arrange your own
celebration for the couple.

Real MoBs:

Making the peace

'I was really disappointed when Sue said she and Joe were going to marry in the Seychelles – so many people would miss out on the event. But we had a huge party on their return, which made up for it.'

Check it's legal!

Do some homework. Make sure your daughter has been properly advised and has made the necessary arrangements. Find out exactly what is required in terms of visas, paperwork and so on for the wedding to be legally valid. A lot of this advice can be found in confetti.co.uk's destination planner at www.confetti.co.uk/travel/finder.asp

Get your jabs done

Find out what vaccinations are needed, if any, and advise others in the wedding party well in advance of the event.

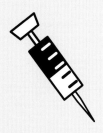

Expect the worst...

Sunburn, diarrhoea, tension headaches. Make sure you've got all the medication you and the wedding party are likely to need, including a well-stocked first aid kit in case of emergencies. If you want to avoid Delhi belly, drink bottled water and avoid ice in drinks. Beware of cold buffets, especially cold meats.

Package the holiday

Make sure you or the bride send an information pack to those travelling with you. This should include details such as the price of hotels and flights, what currency to bring and dress etiquette for the day itself.

Picture the scene

If the wedding will be on a beach, forget
high heels. And make sure your clothes are
suitably cool. Take advice on your make-up
too – you don't want to look shiny-faced
in the wedding pictures.

Family fisticuffs!

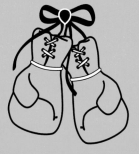

Don't leave it to chance

If certain members of the family don't get on, talk individually to each one and point out your concerns. Chances are, they'll all agree to keep the peace. Have a back-up plan and ask someone reliable to keep an eye out for any signs of conflict.

Must we invite my ex?

If he's the bride's father, it's really down to her whether or not he's included. Try to set aside your feelings for her big day. Talk to him beforehand, and call a truce if you feel it will help you avoid conflict at the wedding.

Too many for top table?

If remarriage means there are now rather
a lot of people to fit on the top table,
don't have one. It's not compulsory.
Or have a round table instead so no
one feels excluded.

YOUR DAUGHTER'S WEDDING

Traditional seating plan

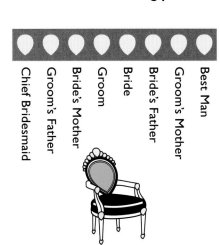

Chief Bridesmaid • Groom's Father • Bride's Mother • Groom • Bride • Bride's Father • Groom's Mother • Best Man

FAMILY FISTICUFFS!

Alternative seating if bride's parents are
divorced and both remarried

Bride's Stepfather

Chief Bridesmaid

Groom's Father

Bride's Mother

Groom

Bride

Bride's Father

Groom's Mother

Best Man

Bride's Stepmother

Keep them apart

Ask your daughter for inside knowledge on any guests who won't get on with each other. Then make sure you separate them on the table plan.

FAMILY FISTICUFFS!

Real MoBs:

The unforgiven

'Miranda hadn't seen her father since he left me. So it was only natural that she should choose me to give her away at the church. No one so much as batted an eyelid.'

Dealing with
difficult daughters

Calm down

Emotions are bound to be running high, but don't let her frayed nerves or temper tantrums get to you.

Calm down

Walk away. Take a deep breath, talk
to a friend – whatever it takes to avoid
an angry confrontation.

When Mr Right is Mr Wrong

So you don't like her fiancé? Try to get to know him better. Concentrate on his positive aspects rather than simply seeing someone you don't consider good enough for your daughter.

Gulp! How much?

Stick to your budget. If your daughter throws a wobbly and insists on something beyond it, suggest she and the groom pay something toward the costs.

Real MoBs:

We compromised

'Jess decided she didn't want any bridesmaids. I thought she was being really unfair on her younger sister. In the end we compromised – her sister was an usher and sat at the top table.'

It's your day too!

What do I do on the day?

If you're following tradition, you arrive with
the bridesmaids or a male relative around
10 minutes before the bride, and are
escorted up the aisle by the chief usher.

Are you receiving me?

Traditionally, the mother of the bride heads
up the receiving line at the reception
venue. The line-up goes as follows: you,
bride's father, groom's mother, groom's
father, bride and groom, best man
and bridesmaids.

Real MoBs:
Things change

'We didn't bother with a receiving line. But once the speeches were over, my husband and I made sure we sat at each table talking to all the guests. We felt that way we had more time to spend with them.'

Delegate duties

You can't be everywhere at once. So if Uncle Ted is known for his alcohol-fuelled political rows, pick a relative to keep an eye on him during the reception.

Planning a speech?

Make sure you have more than one copy of it, just to be on the safe side. Prompt cards with a brief reminder of what you want to say will be very useful, and can easily fit inside a normal-sized handbag.

Practise makes perfect

The more familiar you are with your speech the better, so practise in front of a mirror. Or rehearse it with a sympathetic friend, asking for honest feedback. And don't gabble – speak more slowly than normal so that everyone can hear.

Smile!

This is your day too. The guests are more likely to enjoy it if you're looking happy and relaxed. So even if there's a minor hiccup, keep your cool, smile and, if necessary, take a moment in the Ladies to compose yourself.

Worse for wear

Keep an eye on older relatives getting tired or wobbly on their feet. They might need to be taken home early or given a room they can rest in, especially if it's very hot. Appoint someone (not you!) to keep an eye on them.

IT'S YOUR DAY TOO!

After the tears

Treat yourself. Once you've waved your daughter off on her honeymoon, take a holiday yourself. You know you deserve it!

ABOUT CONFETTI.CO.UK

Confetti.co.uk is the UK's leading weddings
and special occasion website, helping more
than 300,000 brides, grooms and guests
every month.
To find out more or to order your confetti
gift book, party brochure or wedding
stationery brochure, visit www.confetti.co.uk
email info@confetti.co.uk
visit Confetti, 80 Tottenham Court Road,
London W1 or call 0870 840 6060

Some of the other books in this
comprehensive series: *The Best Man's
Wedding*, *The Bridesmaid's Wedding*,
Men At Weddings, and *Wedding Planner*